D0297215

SPORTING HEROES

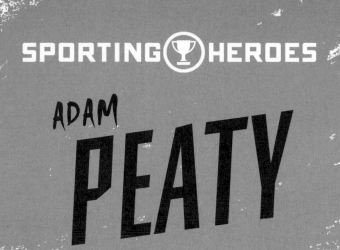

ADAM PEATY

ROY APPS

ILLUSTRATED BY ALESSANDRO VALDRIGHI

LONDON·SYDNEY

Franklin Watts
First published in Great Britain in 2017
by The Watts Publishing Group

Text © Roy Apps 2017
Illustrations © Watts Publishing Group 2017
Illustrator: Alessandro Valdrighi
Cover design: Peter Scoulding
Executive Editor: Adrian Cole

*The statistics in this book were correct at the time
of printing, but because of the nature of the sport,
it cannot be guaranteed that they are now accurate.*

HB ISBN 978 1 4451 5330 8
PB ISBN 978 1 4451 5333 9
Library ebook ISBN 978 1 4451 5332 2

1 3 5 7 9 10 8 6 4 2

Printed in China

Franklin Watts
An imprint of
Hachette Children's Group
Part of The Watts Publishing Group
Carmelite House
50 Victoria Embankment
London EC4Y 0DZ

An Hachette UK Company
www.hachette.co.uk

www.franklinwatts.co.uk

6

7

8

9

CHAPTER TWO
GALA TIME

A couple of weeks later, Adam's mum's friend Marilyn called round to take Adam back to the swimming pool.

'Here's his towel and swimming stuff,' said Adam's mum.

'Oh, we won't want that today. We'll just watch.'

Marilyn took Adam and sat in the viewing gallery, watching and laughing at the other children in the pool.

When the children left the pool, Adam and Marilyn joined them in the café. They had squash and biscuits. Adam quite enjoyed himself.

The following week, Adam and Marilyn went down to the side of the pool to watch the other children swimming. A few weeks after that, Adam was in the pool himself. He wasn't sure whether he liked the water or not, particularly when he got his face wet.

'It's all wet!' he complained.

'That's water for you, Adam!'

He may not have liked getting his face wet, but he did like swimming.

When he went swimming with the school, he found he was one of the fastest.

'He's a big, strong lad,' his teacher told his mum. 'He should do really well in the local schools' swimming gala.'

'Swimming gala?' said his mum, amazed. 'Our Adam?'

Adam did well in the gala, winning each race he was in.

'I can't believe it!' said his mum. 'We had to drag you kicking and screaming to the swimming pool when you were little. And even then we couldn't get you in the water!'

Adam's success in the local schools' swimming gala led to him being selected for a trial at the local Dove Valley swimming club. It was here that he first began swimming in proper competitions.

Mind you, he still hated taking a shower. He made a habit of keeping his head down, so that his face didn't get wet.

CHAPTER THREE
SOMETHING SPECIAL

By the time Adam was at secondary school, he was swimming regularly. He was in the school team, and was winning all his races.

One day, when he was in Year 10, his swimming teacher spoke to him. Adam had just swum in a local schools' event.

'Well done, Adam.'

'Thanks,' replied Adam.

'I think you're good enough to become a top swimmer,' said his teacher.

Adam frowned. He already was a top swimmer. He was the best swimmer in his school, wasn't he?

'I don't mean just being the best in the school,' his swimming teacher said, as if reading his thoughts. 'I mean swimming competitively at regional and national level. How does that sound?'

'Cool,' said Adam.

'Of course, it would mean joining one of the large swimming clubs. Derby would be a good choice—'

'Derby?' exclaimed Adam. 'That's miles away from Uttoxeter!'

'It's the best,' his swimming teacher replied.

Adam frowned. It seemed like a big step.

'How about I take you there for a trial?'

On the way to Derby, Adam's swimming teacher explained: 'The head coach at Derby is Mel Marshall.'

Adam was impressed. 'I've heard of her. She was in the Olympic swimming team in Beijing.'

His teacher nodded. 'She's also got six Commonwealth Gold medals.'

CHAPTER FOUR
THE BIG DECISION

Mel sat with Adam and his parents at home in their sitting room.

'If Adam's going to make it to the top — and he's got the talent — it'll mean big changes for you all.'

'How do you mean?' asked Adam's dad.

'Adam's going to have to get up early for a start.'

'There's no problem with that, is there son?' Adam's dad asked him. Adam's dad worked as a caretaker in a supermarket, and was used to getting up early.

'By early I mean 4.30am,' added Mel.

Adam's jaw dropped. 'Half past four! Are you serious? Why?'

'To get in a couple of hours training before you go to school. The swimmers I coach train at Repton School pool. It's 25 metres long. The best around here.'

So, each morning, at half past four, Adam's mum drove him to the pool at Repton. It was about forty minutes away. As Adam sat in bleary silence in

the car, it seemed to him as if it was the middle of the night.

After Adam's early morning training session, his mum drove him to school. Then she headed to work. After school, his mum drove him back to Repton. There he had another training session.

The training sessions were expensive. Plus, it cost about £100 a week in petrol to get Adam to training and back.

He trained hard though, and his dedication paid off. At the 2010 Midland Youth Championships, he won gold in the Men's 15—16 years 50 metre breaststroke. He won the 100 metre breaststroke, too. He also took home silver in the 200 metre breaststroke.

But focusing on becoming a top swimmer meant that Adam missed out on doing other stuff with his mates.

'Coming out tonight, Adam?'

'Thought we'd go to a party.'

'Nah, better not. I've got to be up at half past four tomorrow.'

'All work and no play, Adam...'

Gradually, though, Adam began to go out more and more with his mates. He would get back late and miss training the next morning.

'I'm seventeen; I'm not a kid any more,' he thought. It didn't take too long for his swimming to suffer.

Then, one evening, Adam was getting ready for another late night with his mates. While he waited for them, he watched highlights of the 2012 London Olympics on TV. There was a familiar face in one of the swimming events...

CHAPTER FIVE
BURN THE BOATS

The following year, Adam was busy training for the 2014 Commonwealth Games. Mel noticed that he seemed quite glum.

'What's wrong, Adam?'

Adam shrugged. 'Oh... It's all happened so quickly. It wasn't long ago that I was doing only Youth Championships, and now here I am, planning to compete with the best swimmers in the world.'

Mel frowned. 'I thought you were worried about something. You're great in the heats, but you always seem to struggle to produce your fastest time in the finals.'

CHAPTER SIX
RECORD BREAKER

At the 2014 Commonwealth Games, Adam stood on the side of the pool. He was waiting for the starting signal for the 50 metres breaststroke final.

To help him concentrate, he formed a picture in his mind. A picture of Alexander the Great burning his boats.

'Attack!' Adam muttered to himself. 'Attack!'

As soon as the starting signal sounded, Adam was away. Any nerves were instantly drowned with one thought — attack.

He came in just 0.02 seconds behind the winner, South African Cameron van der Burgh (the Olympic Champion and World record holder). In the 100 metres, 19-year-old Adam broke the British record to win gold, ahead of Cameron van der Burgh in second place.

Now the talk was of only one thing: preparing for the 2016 Olympic Games.

'It all feels a bit crazy,' Adam admitted to Mel. 'It's like a dream. Cameron was my idol — he still is, I suppose — and now he's my biggest rival.'

In 2015, Adam broke the world 100 metres breaststroke record. He took almost half a second off! He was the first swimmer ever to swim 100 metres breaststroke in under 58 seconds.

Later that year, at the FINA World Aquatic Championships, he broke the 100 metres breaststroke world record not once, but twice. He was a World Champion. Now, the pressure was really on him to do well at the 2016 Olympics.

'The history of Olympic swimming is full of world champions who flunk it in the Olympic pool,' Adam thought to himself. 'Supposing I turn out to be another one of them?'

CHAPTER SEVEN
AN UNLIKELY SPONSOR

'What do you mean, you won't be in Rio to watch me?'

Adam sat in the sitting room with his mum and dad. His dad sighed.

'It's like your mum said, Adam. There's no way we can afford it. Two thousand pounds each just for the flights out there. And the cheapest hotels start at a hundred and fifty pounds a night.'

Adam sat there, stunned. He understood that his parents hadn't got the money to go to Rio; he knew they weren't rich. In the early days, it had been a struggle to find the money for petrol to get him to Derby for training.

But whenever he'd raced, either his mum or dad — and sometimes both of them — had been there. And however big or noisy the crowd, Adam had always thought he could hear them cheering,

'Go, Adam! Go!'

His family were a core part of 'Team Peaty'. The Rio Olympics would be the first time no one from his family was there to support him.

'Oh, and another thing,' Adam's mum added, glumly. 'I haven't been able to wash your towels and stuff. The washing machine's packed up.'

A few days later the washing machine repair man called round to the Peaty's house. He looked up and saw a photo of Adam on the wall.

'I thought the name was familiar,' he said. 'That's Adam Peaty, the swimmer, isn't it?'

Adam's dad nodded. 'Our son.'

'My little girl's just started swimming. She loves it.'

The washing machine repair man got started with his spanners. 'You must be looking forward to going to Rio.'

'I don't think we'll be able to go,' Adam's mum explained. 'We just don't have that sort of money.'

When the washing machine repair man got back to the depot, he told his manager how the Peatys wouldn't be able to go to Rio. The manager called head office.

'Adam Peaty. The young swimmer. He's in need of a bit of sponsorship — at least, his family are. Do you think the company could help?'

'I think we could,' said the lady at head office. 'Swimming... washing machines... it's all about water, after all.'

Later that day, Adam's dad's phone rang.

'Mr Peaty? Domestic & General here. Washing machine repairs? We'd like to become Team Peaty sponsors. We can help with the costs of getting you and your family to Rio.'

CHAPTER EIGHT
GOING FOR GOLD

Thanks to the washing machine company, Adam's family were able to travel to Rio for the 2016 Olympic Games. By the time the games opened, Adam was favourite to win gold.

'It's yours for the taking,' people kept telling him.

Adam wished they wouldn't. It just piled on the pressure.

In the 100 metres breaststroke heats, he won in 57.62 seconds, breaking his own world record of 57.88 seconds, which he had set the year before. He eased through the semi-final. The question was, could he beat the reigning World Champion, Cameron van der Burgh, in the final?

Everyone knew Adam suffered from nerves. Would the butterflies in his stomach mean him getting off to a slow start?

Adam strode out to the edge of the pool with the other finalists. He felt his chest tightening with nerves. Briefly, he shut his eyes; formed a picture in his mind. A now familiar image of Alexander the Great burning all his boats.

'Attack!' Adam muttered to himself.

There were a few shouts from the crowd. One yell stood out from all the others:

'Go, Adam! Go!'

Then they were under starter's orders, 'Take your marks...' BEEP!

Adam's start was incredible. He shot into the pool and powered forward, with van der Burgh right there with him. At the turn, though, Adam was leading. As he stormed into the final 25 metres, it was clear that another world record was about to be smashed.

By the time he touched the pool side, his nearest rival, Cameron van der Burgh, was more than a body length behind him.

Adam punched the water in delight, before shaking the water from his face and congratulating his fellow competitors. It was only then that he glanced up at the race clock: 57.13 seconds.

57.13 seconds? An almost impossible time. He'd broken his own world record — again!

Adam gazed up and smiled at the cheering crowd. He looked around. There they were, the special faces; his dad, his mum, his girlfriend Anna and his coach Mel Marshall: Team Peaty.

Adam stood on the podium to receive his first Olympic gold medal — and Team GB's first gold medal of the 2016 Olympic Games.

SPORTING 🏆 HEROES

FACT FILE

Full name: Adam Peaty

Date of birth: 28th December 1994

Place of birth: Uttoxeter, Staffordshire, UK

Height: 1.91m (6ft 3in)

Club: City of Derby

GLOSSARY

Alexander the Great — Alexander III (CE 356—323) was King of Macedonia and conqueror of the Persian Empire

FINA — International Swimming Federation, the official organisation responsible for organising swimming events

gala — a sports meeting

heats — a set of races held to determine who goes through to the next round

podium — a platform on which athletes stand for the medal presentations

relay — a race in which several athletes take part in different legs or stages of the same length

rival — a direct competitor

stroke — the style of swimming: backstroke, breaststroke, butterfly and freestyle

CAREER

Key Medals:

Men's 100 metres breaststroke

World Aquatics Championships, gold medal	2017
Olympic Games, gold medal	2016
European Championships, gold medal	2016
World Aquatics Championships, gold medal	2015
Commonwealth Games, gold medal	2014
European Aquatics Championships, gold medal	2014

Men's 50 metres breaststroke

World Aquatics Championships, gold medal	2017
World Aquatics Championships, gold medal	2015
European Aquatics Championships, gold medal	2014

World Records:

50 metres breaststroke:	25.95 seconds
100 metres breaststroke:	57.13 seconds
4 x 100 metre mixed medley relay:	3:41.71

Other Achievements:

• Adam is the first swimmer ever to win both the 100 metres and 50 metres breaststroke events at the same World Aquatics Championships.

• He is the most successful British swimmer in a single World Championships.

• He is the only British swimmer to have won gold medals at Olympic, World, European and Commonwealth Games level, in the same event at the same time.

• Adam was awarded an MBE (Most Excellent Order of the British Empire) by the Queen in 2016.

SPORTING  HEROES

Greg was sixteen when athletics coach Tom McNab invited him to join an elite group of promising young athletes in his home town of Milton Keynes. Joining the group didn't come cheap — it cost £200 a month — but somehow Greg's parents found the money, even though they weren't well off.

Greg still had his taste for late nights, clubbing and fast cars, though...

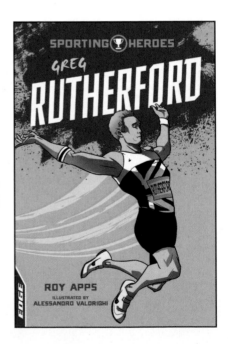

CONTINUE READING
GREG RUTHERFORD'S
AMAZING STORY IN...